the eclipse

advance praise

"Jay Smith shows us, with absolute clarity, how poetry, maybe *only* poetry, can express the baffling array of overlapping contradictions running through life in late capitalism. With a persistent and yet subtle procedurality, she manages to give us snapshots of a world where industrialists sidle up to nymphs, dresses are objects, and art and nature exist in and apart from the monochrome steel of contemporary life. Only a lifelong student and now master of language could produce poems as masterfully lyrical and architectural as these."
—Lori Emerson, associate professor University of Colorado at Boulder and founder of the Media Archaeology Lab, a museum dedicated to obsolete technologies

"*The Eclipse* slows down the reel of film to its component frames and out of them arranges a collage of intensified images of modern urban life: concrete, steel, exhaust, the structures and machinations of gender. In this collection, reflections slide and pierce, economies and affects merge, and representation and image are layered over themselves again and again. With a Benjaminian call—'let us transpose / art on art'—these sharp poems bring our attention to the practice of looking again, and of noticing which narratives look back."
—Jason Purcell, author of *Swollening*

"Jay Smith's new collection is a true marvel: to find oneself once more immersed in Antonioni's world of images and signs is a novel, surprising, revitalizing experience. These are poems rich in visual and narrative echoes and allusions, as well as compelling ventures in rhythm and irony with a tenor and impetus all of their own."
—Laura Rascaroli, professor of film and screen media at University College Cork and editor of *Antonioni: Centenary Essays*.

the eclipse

poems after antonioni

m. jay smith

IGUANA

Publisher: Cheryl Hawley
Editor: Lee Parpart

ISBN 978-1-77180-683-1 (paperback)

This is an original print edition of *the eclipse*.

contents

do as images do

the industrialist's daughter

snaps fingers at empty air
opens the sudden space of habit

to the wind. an unfurling story

hangs mid-air, softening to myth

or the rhythms of city,
this porosity walked over. think of

thought as
a concrete slab strung to

electrical wires, its bright waves
shedding light & glancing live

connection

when in cinema, do as
images do: unfurl comparisons,

hold up sleek surfaces like woman or
architecture. reverberate

juxtaposition. these reflections

pierce geography. in the gasp of the
now, seeing is voluptuousness

& the lush monochrome city
gleams miraculously, economically

in units of time & resource development.
now rhetoric exceeds the bucket

list that brought it to the party. rhetoric won't
dance nicely with its date anymore. that

glimmer of steel &
dimension took its breath away

in a contempt of heart ache
remember bankers & the sundress
with blossoms on it

this is the brutalism of economic
miracles: the girth of raw

concrete, ascending lines & opportunity flush with
industrialists

whose fat fingers pulse urbanely,
tips streaming

with light towards the
constellations of evening

& city, robust & glittering amidst
that enveloping amber glow

landscape unfurls:
grass, cooling tower, sky

watch how use value
obeys teleological principles, how

flat surfaces break the alphabet of
erosion & grasses

woman, be the flesh
of transformation. there is this

black dress

architecture is a thick centrality
rising in a perfect arc & whose

glassiness then pitches & falls off

while those thick-necked industrialists
create the wealth,

objects that resist temporality

that crisp white shirt coaxing the roses from
the bush, snipping at the best blooms

it is a wellspring of open
ness: who speaks of wealth when this

is what abundance *is*, a pouring
over, a flock of a lot but still too few

pretty women in little black dresses
or like a bush full of roses

semiosis is the leisure class

& if wealth sheds an object, a thing
of itself to be known

fine finery for the tautological class
a silver sliver of a coin

in a wallet hitched high to the inner thigh
& other wealth-begetting

adornments: a silk dress, a clatter of
heels on tile, a language that

transposes fiction to upper management

or landscape architecture whose
shrubbery is a manicure,

a horse dancing & biting at the
bit, a woman who knows what

she wants & how to refrain from
wanting it

for what begets nostalgia
begets beauty. what churns

progress ignites a cartoon
revelation, a slap of lightning

across the forehead

& *il miracolo economico*. this is a
category of genesis, of begetting, it is

the baser wonder of resource

narrative is an erasure, languidly announced,
a record re-recording mantras

and observations
throughout time. this repetition

is porosity & it
fattens with a celluloid nostalgia

where the domain of identical women
is set against fields or glamorous

cities, where class is a blunt sentiment,
where forms

build solidity softly & march toward

an intemperate future

all the nymphs

the delta of industry

& the nymphs have departed

(a wasteland is a wasteland)

empty bottles, sandwich papers, silk
handkerchiefs, cardboard boxes, cigarette ends

these fragments have shored up

& everything was singing, everything

under the brown fog of a winter dawn

the sky is full of constellations

full of pump jacks & scaffolding

men talking in telephone games

& the semiotics of swagger

industrial manhood thunders:
plumes of steam, hands in suit pockets,

chit chat wired frenetic & so
important

plume is the language of
a seismic aesthetic

like the exoskeleton of miracle

a painted square, rothko, painted
grass. pipeline

cathedral. the eye has to

wander.

or garbage & fruit: the primordia of
cityscape is factory

plumes of steam billow / the beginning of time

this handpainted world, grasses
& garbage & fruit

civilization has thirst

the nostalgia of blue nighttime,

our chiaroscuro
lapse of sky

americana is the skyline on the cuff, the collar,

cuff links chattering against brick

the spray-painted world in monochrome

occupies space between a man &
a woman. like how

subjectivity condenses in a cloud
in billowing plumes

a jet of pressure

the afternoon of duck eggs & flasks

this tailings pond, the beach house
of bad-toothed couples,

balding & broken boards

on the mountain brim of horizon
woman is ephemeral,

just the exhaust of lingering

looking beauty by the fireplace, feet
outstretched & nylon

here is only pump jacks & empty fields,
polluted streams & mutant fish

& those empty skies: small spaces are naive

here, fat fingers excite the fabric of
a green sweater

negozio, negozio

the soft grind of metal
on metal thrums & whirrs, dreams

geometric dreams:

iron spheres, concrete cylinders, steel pipes

these angles of glorious refinement & metal, rising
from this barren patch. th'engines are primed

& blazing red diodes illuminate every
shadowing. what need is elemental,

this whirr across the room, fore & aft,
a din in the background growing soft & grey

a flannel forgetfulness, fore & aft, landscape
diffusing its soft mechanical plumes to the sky

a woman sings a woman's voice

ô cassandra, ô giuliana

la notte

the modern woman, unabbreviated

peels the crust of black from a

black wall. through

palisades of distraction or
destruction,

modernism & clean lines.
consider these surfaces of glass

where reflections slide
on fissures of love

& things unbroken are now encrusted,
peeling away, but do not feel

sad there is still a sleek distance that arcs
skywards,

take as landscape, the supposition of

industrialists & the rhythm of
cities: the concrete power

ticks from
mechanism & production

when art flourishes, steel & glass
flourish: the texture of gentrification

is smooth
& the future unfurls vigour

in a pivot of thighs:
ennui is uneconomical

nostalgia lurks on pavement
spells staccato paths;

detour beyond cityscape
to blank fields where

boys shoot rocket plumes skyward,
brawl childishly

shirtless & impassioned

the myth of origin
lives in cheap diners where —

on cobblestone streets where —
under trees beneath which —

& grasses

the technology of the familiar,
in new landscapes,

begets soft declaratives:
a country estate *is*

as if wealth is without
substance, erasures

poolside, amidst the bloom of
roses, as if

luxury evanesces in the vapour of
cigarettes, & similarly

prescriptive relations of art

(base & superstructure,
baby

fidelity purses the woman of the mid-
summer night

cleaving textures of her black silk &
monochrome gloss. her elision is

implausible rain that distorts
the given & now the sadness of

wet & mirrors
is creeping back in. for

denotation is a string of pearls
amidst perambulations

& all liquids appear as gases or espresso,
perhaps wine. these

objects embed narrative

all the empty rooms are party
scenes reflected in the soft

equilibrium of glass
while selfhood rebounds against

selfhood in narratives & board games

& industriousness whispers sweetly
in glistening ears

about social relations, about
pearls & things that glitter, ink &

wellsprings of wealth, about grasses
undulating dutifully

il miracolo economico

the band plays the mourning dull
cracks of grey dawn break

bleak meadows & dewy grey grass
couch forgotten love letters

heroism is suave, a tactful ego

& all the empty fields are party scenes
reflected in the soft equilibrium of glass

haunted by something stronger
than habit or time; the familiar is

vastly monochrome & soaked in

deciduous regrets

l'avventura

ricca ragazza romana scomparsa a lisca bianca

seaborne, yachtbound

the sky ambles vastness

bracket, encapsulate
condense, display

ô
this surfeit of landscape

below deck, a woman
assembles a jigsaw of
landscape

gaps fill with
interlocking pieces

here is nature
in the image
of nature

meaning, or the
newspaper thrown flutteringly
into the wake

the represented object vibrates at
the expense of dogma

the balm of weather
in late summer
on a pleasure craft

woman, man. bikini.
frilly swim cap

how naked bellies
smack hard against waves

& then goneness resonates,
settles as habit.

adventures unfurl. as
story.

delve into
the space between things,
a button-up blouse, a diamond
ring

while viscera plummet
to glance over cliffs &
nothing smashes on rocks

how scuba divers plunge
beneath the chopping surface

the sequence of not-forgetting

splashes, thrashes, aligns
with coterminous
desire

in a foggy luminosity,
we are numinous
beauty.

we percolate direction through
misdirection

we find that
lost is a tremendous
unfinding

here are fields of rock
& the wind

let us transpose
art on art, or
the female nude

clothes make the woman
an economy

a shirt for a shirt
a dress for a dress

which shall i wear?
this one, or this one?

once objects mastered sly
transformations, pressed against
skin, an ill-fitting

cardigan a frumpy wool
skirt

what   transitions is
luxury: a thing of

pure aesthetic. or triumph

the resolute
beauty of tautology:

a bauble is a bauble
is a bauble

testify to
these baubles in a box.

a ring on a finger.

the distance of appraisal,
the length of an arm.

look how the self is
objective beauty.

folded over, witness to it-
self.

here is leisure:
it clatters as
black pumps on ceramic tile.

as a lofty
patio glistens white
against its chiaroscuro sky.

it is as meticulous
as those things, just as
harmonious.

hermeneutic activities
of the leisure class

the car has arrived.

beneath the patio &
the sky,

pedestrians
submit to terrain.

peal the self against
dimensions. for instance, how

no thought is quite
as durable as
woman. or how

spaghetti straps
in the evening cling
lustfully

art is
a plunging
want

bracket, encapsulate,
condense, display.

a man
suckles a painted breast. what

outrageous cliché is the woman,

hand
on a white pillowcase. how

irreplaceable

(implacable)

what fidelity / what a slut

here is
nature in the image of
nature

sei la luce dei miei occhi

polysemy compares the apple
of your eye

to the sun. this body tied in
muscles, freckles:

words undo
temporality's certain closeness to the

sun. the idea
of flesh takes on real thirst: this patch of grass,

fir trees, a beam of sunlight

count fewer trees
where sylvan reveries

brim to the highway's edge
nostalgia is

not made to scale, is
unmeasured by the handspan

of humans. no, mountains obey the
tautology of mountainous things:

remember that now

renew the tautology that brings us
ever closer to

semiotics's crocheted approach to the
thing itself. much
love is just

a sequential evaporation,

denser than the needle-
springy ground, cloudier than

the sky

let's evade the
obvious, the not quite

brush of skin against skin &
of course it is an economy:

a surface for a surface.
a likeness looks

likely when a kiss trades on
a coax of temerity,

a dyadic yearn
the hub of a long ascent

the opposite of utility is rocks
lake trees mountain is

taste. what common denominators are
beauty! a man! a freckle of

skin! his musculature is the
broad shoulder of beauty!

that sunbeam or the delineation of—

the eclipse

the mind connects
constellations, star-crossed
love

like becomes like
whereas

genre billows a white shift:
a woman holding fossilized grass

& all the want to want of a man
many telephones that ring
sonorously

& when the market in a nice suit
seeks transcendence,

numbers flip revelations on the wall

so the self is a dividend of the self

that fills the container that contains
want; a small handbag, a drawer of flowers

on the cobblestone contours of street
vastness is round,

unflagged flagpoles swaying against

the soft percussion of the wind:

temptation shows tensile
strength

grandeur is thought impervious to time

& the concrete of brutalism is
grander than nature

so the civic selves are wondrous
walking through the heroism of cities

so read through grass
varietals on romance, tropes

the man in a nice
suit. the woman in a white blouse
the leaves of the fan palm

brush faces; it is a species of
affection & in these surfaces — a park,

a stalled moment—
an excess of jubilation

& aspirations are concrete, thoughts
shown through glass

like, brutalism is
the harshest plain. pane

confound species
the frenzy of the market, the translation
something for something else

endurance is just a lure, a half-
realized object

so the ground orchestrates a
pleasure, authentically, sounds
like or unlike

the sonority of telephones in an office,
a marketplace, a wrestling ring

the simultaneity of recourse
is astonishing,

how thirst spills out from
the detritus of rain barrels

a piece of wood, an empty match
book. rivulets of passion run
through sand & gravel

there is always another sunset

when a fragile beacon is night:
the crowds
illuminate dusty streets

men in black, women in white
the universe is dyadic, half built

in concrete, beneath the cloudy sky;

look
how geometry vanishes into distance
& thirst unwashes age

the spume of leisure

something
resembles something else

polarized sentiment is
this, spume

& we set our sights on waves:

on endless undulations:

on whales, the language of sand,
on markers of snail & seed

the mind makes substitutions

undo the substance of what is
quotidian:

a friction of flesh

thighs heavy & bikini
brief

here be the girth of intersections,
water set upon
water

the aquamarine
waves.

think water the colour
of water or
the sea

a vacation, a pineapple drink

the swim-up bar is just
a semiotic event

our denotata is languid:

palm tree, conch, wave

leisure favourably compares
with leisure

& pure recreation is pure form

& the self is divisible into pure
selves

of leisure or economy

like janus suns th'self;
on the beach chair

the bikini self is laid bare
on towelled futures & sandy

on the second day, the lei
browns &
          on day 3 of paradise,
beetles scurry from the petals

when the humpback smashes &
against waves

tails smack water fleetingly
a trompe-l'oeil charade &

the clouds low & close

clouds that discharge
wet narratives of nature

undulations of substance
contrary to the self

unfamiliar fruit from familiar trees
melons sliced on a platter

small selves are slick
in sunscreen, rain

a lavish porosity, we

hawai'ian musicians in grass skirts
hidden behind a shed smoking

we are elvis
we are aloha

sand dunes are   thick w/
                think of

resort children turn tan
turn fat bellies to the sun

surf, or the elemental conceits

burnished lava, a shoreline, a sun
set in the idyllic hues. what is

essential is contrast, how
tan lines slip from swim suits how

untied from tongues our story
flits & becomes

the self amongst its contemporaries:
smaller selves in sunbeams

substance is lyric &
leisure is lyric:

sand or surf

the red desert

today's dream you dream of
scarves.
utopian shapes

perched on
dirty grass, dimensions
challenging belief:

cathedrals of pipes & valves
a glimmering city

& on the thresholds of wool &
soot, walk down long alleys:

scarves, ceramics

& with all your shoes
this spring saunters

monica vitti, you inhabit
my ceramic reverie. the long
contours of street

sing

tautology's beauty is
a conflation of
blonde & loneliness

here spaciousness reiterates the
fat echo of emptiness circling

a vast nothing
by topography, by the crow's
flight

electrical towers arch their
fragile reach cloudily

muted trombones melt down

that mild disquietude of
woman, a frisson of

taut fibres, woman, i get
it: this sound of being
worth,

listen, there is no numbness akin to

in this patch of flatness where
austerity is the pitch of

nightscape; terror

while frantic bodies perform their
capitulations, dutifully, like to

like to transgression
a domestic tableau

& what sand or granule is this
moment, when accolade hits, plush

when hands reach for the scope
of back

touch is a cobblestone of
curved movement, in units

divisible by time or distance

now urban density is languid: dance
on this slippery surface, buy
painted fruit

the trumpets are bleating
appropriately!

the subject believes in its object, like
the cityscape believes

in you or a soft plume
of fabric, a teacup

& so make the syntax of city
trill: a woman is

an eternal trophy, climate controls
storage, in the manhole
cover of night

we are all descended from
origin myths

& our concrete
lineages are florid,
glistening with tar & rain

so the footprint of materialism
is sandstone, a galaxy

the snows of kilimanjaro

an incandescent shadow play
between brick apartments

between plaster walls & the neighbours
open windows incant: the murmur of talk

here is the secret power of images
to beget images, new

images in the form of images, wet & newly
pictorial images, untautological clones of images

out in the world, on the cobblestones of images &
images of dogs escaping through the night images

& look at these of dust & racism,

of elephant feet & the snow of distant mountains

the image of the frame on the tabletop
framing the image of the object

picture is already a mimicry economy

this is how image women naturally becomes exotic.
image women is already exotic

how reproducible they is, even bereft of

discriminating taste. look at these images of the
big game hunters! the safari on the savannah!

politics, women, drink, money & ambition
are image. american writers tickle the image of ivories

& look at mountainscape: snow as smooth
to see as cake frosting, image light as powder

the speed & noiseless rush of simile
drops down like a bird image. woman image

smiles. woman image approves

imagine a bellowing of catastrophe sounds

the magnificent bull begets the crashing bear

amidst telephones & screaming, a flurry

& the speculative subject merges

with the market object. it is transubstantial,
the magical prowess of the fetish

or the stuff of revelation:

numbers flip on the wall, pinning selfhood
to a numerological dictum. economics are

so emotional. the meek pose
smoking cigarettes by marble pillars, tapping

housewifely slingbacks on marble floors,
the nothingness of new debt is

tangible, on slips of small papers, or flowers

do not underestimate the wind
rustling through dark deciduous boughs

the reclusiveness of brick, bamboo
blinds & scaffolding. the half-

built now entreats,

man is the cockiness of springtime & fields,
the wealth of dark chambers & this offering

a box of empty chocolates

the plenitude of what flesh is substance

belongs to him, beyond semiosis,

the energy of chimes or flagpoles that
undulate soft percussion in the wind

wonder is this pedestal in the night, purely
generated of miracles like

material, marble, the mysterious thrum of self,
cobblestones that glisten frenetically

peak oil is peak happiness

where bliss smears against windows &
gauze, when kisses are duplicate images

reflected or deliberately reproduced
ad infinitum. brink until the ink

is dry. love is the threshold of love

the market reflects a sound industrial situation

& liquidity is still very high, the lips are still very
moist. meaning in a system of exchange

is glossy. call the call girl. once you get used to
the arbitrariness of signs,

it becomes a passion

now night has broken into
constituent elements

unchosen couples spill from a bus

trees undulate
the leaves of dark & passion

in the rustle & scope of foliage, a rain
barrel whose spilling rivulets

fail to slake the dust &
thirst. how narrative rebounds & pulls on a line:

expect that blonde, that man
in a suit & his swagger, & still, wait

acknowledgements

This book grew out of poems that I workshopped with Erín Moure while she served as writer in residence at the University of Alberta in 2014 and 2015. I'm grateful to have had the opportunity to learn poetic methods from such a legend of Canadian poetics. Much later, I benefitted immensely from the excellent editorial eye of Lee Parpart at Iguana Books. Thanks to Greg Iouannou for his advocacy and good humour. Heather Chontos kindly let me use her art for the cover image. My family, especially Gabi and Milo, endure me. As does Robin. Big love.

Printed in the USA
CPSIA information can be obtained
at www.ICGtesting.com
JSHW021449091124
73279JS00003B/50

9 781771 806831